ANOTHER 500 ALL TIME FUNNIEST GOLF JOKES, STORIES & FAIRWAY WISDOM

Sheila & Ron Stewart

ANOTHER 500 ALL TIME FUNNIEST GOLF JOKES, STORIES & FAIRWAY WISDOM

ISBN: 0-9656856-2-4

Published by

Acadia Scale Press

Books by Sheila & Ron Stewart

500 All Time Funniest Golf Jokes, Stories & Fairway Wisdom

500 More All Time Funniest Golf Jokes, Stories & Fairway Wisdom

Another 500 All Time Funniest Golf Jokes, Stories & Fairway Wisdom

500 All Time Funniest *Slightly Off The Fairway* Golf Jokes, Stories & Fairway Wisdom

500 All Time Funniest *Husband & Wife* Golf Jokes, Stories & Fairway Wisdom

500 All Time Funniest *Almost On The Green* Golf Jokes, Stories & Fairway Wisdom

500 All Time Funniest *All Over The Golf Course* Golf Jokes, Stories & Fairway Wisdom

Dogs & Clouds & Love & Life

The Professor Murders

The Sandstorm Connection

**For Paul, Donna, Dorothy, D.C.,
Sandy, Muriel, Jack, Wendy, Helen, Ross,
Shirley, Bob & Maureen.**

ANOTHER 500
ALL TIME FUNNIEST
GOLF JOKES,
STORIES
& FAIRWAY WISDOM

Husband: "I accidentally hit something with my golf ball today."
Wife: "What?"
Husband: "A fairway."

When I prepare to putt I try to picture in my mind my ball rolling across the green and falling into the cup. I don't recall my mind picturing my ball rolling off the green and into the lake.

"I use the same technique to remember the accuracy of my golf score that I use to remember people. What was your name again?"

The nice part about golf is, no matter how much a course aggravates us, we can always find another course that will aggravate us even more.

I finally shot 18 good holes of golf . . . and it only took me three and a half years to do it.

"My husband wanted to tell me about his entire golf game, but I said that all I required was a description of the first two holes."
"Why just two holes?"
"I needed to get to sleep early."

Nobody is happier than a golfer with a good disposition. On the other hand, nobody is grumpier than a golfer with a bad disposition.

On the first hole a golfer took seven shots and gave himself a par. On the second hole he took eight shots and again gave himself a par. After watching this for most of the round, another golfer commented, "If it takes him that many shots to get a par, imagine how many it must take him to get a birdie."

Minister at funeral: "We gather here today to say a fond farewell to Henry McAllister."
Congregation: "Amen."
Minister: "As you all know, Henry was a golfer, and he passed away where he would have wanted, on the golf course he loved so much."
Congregation: "Amen."
Minister: "In fact, Henry's final act of love on this earth was to pull out his trusty driver and hit a towering drive more than 300 yards straight down the middle of the fairway."
Congregation: "Amen."
Voice from rear of congregation: "I wonder where I could get one of those drivers."

A golfer who had been hit by a ball was being looked after by the club pro. After making sure he was all right, the pro picked up the golfer's hat which was made of green and yellow tartan with a large furry red ball on the top, and said, "You should never give them a target."

"What was your final score?"
"96, but that could change."
"How could it possibly change?"
"My husband is examining my score card."

If golf is supposed to be therapeutic, why do so many golfers look like they could use therapy.

"What do you think about me making a 200 yard drive across this lake?" one golfer asked another. "That depends," the other golfer replied. "Did you just do it or are you about to try it?"

"My short game really looked good today," a husband said to his wife upon returning home from a golf game. "Unfortunately, I was playing it off the tee."

"I canceled my tee time today because of the hurricane and the three inches of rain flooding the fairways."
"And you call yourself a golfer."

"After five years of golf, I don't look at my game in exactly the same way I used to," one golfer informed another.
"What's the difference?" the other golfer asked. "For one thing," the first golfer answered, "I occasionally get to look at it in the fairway."

My wife has started to golf with me, but I don't think she quite understands the concept. When I go golfing I take a golf bag and fourteen clubs. When she goes golfing she takes a golf bag, fourteen clubs, and three suitcases.

If you're keeping track of the scores, never put another golfer down for a ten, even if you're sure that's what he shot on the hole. It could prove embarrassing later when you discover he only gave himself an eight, or a two.

"Didn't I see you in this rough ten minutes ago?"
"Yes you did. I was searching for my first drive."
"Didn't you find it?"
"Yes I did."
"Then why are you still here?"
"Now I'm searching for my second drive."

"I think my husband hit his ball a little farther into the rough than usual."
"What makes you say that?"
"He took the golf course layout map in with him."

"Do you prefer to charge the pin or lay up on this hole?" one golfer asked another.
"I prefer to charge the pin," the other golfer answered. "However, my ball usually prefers to lay up. We just can't seem to agree on where it's going to lay up at."

"Do you ever get excited when you hit a good shot?" a golfer was asked.
"I'm sure I would," he replied, "if I ever did."

"I discovered there are 104 different ways to hit a golf ball."
"How do you know that?"
"I used them all in my game this morning."

Two golfers were watching as a third thrashed away in a sand trap. After many fruitless efforts without getting his ball out, he charged in circles, swearing and beating his club against the earth.
"Would you mind telling me why we took up this game?" one of the onlookers commented.
"I think it was because someone said it would relax us and relieve our frustrations," the other answered.

Two birds were sitting in a tree, watching a foursome of golfers.
"What seems to be the point of the game?" one bird asked.
"I'm not sure," the other bird answered, "but I think they get points for hitting their ball into that long grass below us, or into that lake over there. Most of them are really good at it too, except every once in a while they miss and hit that short grass in the middle."

I used to get upset because I hit so many poor golf shots, until my golf instructor told me to go to the club house, have a refreshment, and relax. It worked. I haven't hit a bad shot since. It's difficult to hit a bad shot from the club house.

"Golfers on this course play by winter rules, which allow them to move their ball to improve a lie."
"Really? And when do the winter rules end?"
"The preceding season's winter rules generally run until sometime in July."
"Why July?"
"Because that's when the next season's winter rules go into effect."

First golfer: "I used to shoot golf in the nineties, until my wife said that I should get out and play more, and now my score is in the seventies."
Second golfer: "I wish I had a score like that."
Third golfer: "I wish I had a wife like that."

"Those are not strokes," one golfer said to another as he thrashed away at his ball in deep rough. "I was just clearing the grass away from around my ball."

"I'm a little concerned about where my ball might have landed after what that home owner said to me," one golfer confided to another as he looked over a fence to see where his errant drive had gone.
"Oh? What did he say?"
"You have the right to remain silent . . . ."

"The last time I played this golf course, I almost hit some ducks that were on a green."
"I didn't know that."
"You didn't know there were ducks on this golf course?"
"I didn't know you could hit a green."

"There's a fellow in this club house bar who improves our golf game every time we talk to him," an old timer said to a beginner.
"Wow! I'd like to meet him," the beginner exclaimed. "Do you think he could improve my game?"
"He certainly can," the old timer replied. "In fact, I guarantee it. Just a moment and I'll get him for you. Oh waiter, another round please."

"My last drive traveled at least 350 yards."
"What did you do that was different?"
"Nothing really. Once my ball hit the concrete in the parking lot, it just seemed to take off . . . ."

"What do you mean, my ball sailed 175 yards and landed in the lake," a husband exclaimed to his wife. "That ball sailed 250 yards if it moved an inch."

I have to stop letting my wife keep score. She can't keep her mind on the game. Yesterday she gave me a birdie, two pars, six bogeys, a dozen eggs, milk, jam, and don't forget to buy shoes for the kids.

Slicing is a lot like yawning. Once you see someone else do it, you have to do it.

A golfer asked if he could play in the foursome that followed his ex-wife's foursome. When asked why, he answered, "It improves my aim."

A question on the application form to join the local county club read, "Average Score - if a golfer?"
"72," the applicant wrote.
"That's a really low average," he was told. "Are you sure your score is that low?"
"I'm sure it would be," he replied. "If I were a golfer."

"How was golf with your father today?" a mother asked her teenage son.
"O.K., but he's a little angry with me," the son answered.
"Why?"
"Because he said to watch his swing and hit my ball where he hit his ball, and I didn't."
"Where did you hit your ball?"
"The fairway."

"See that dog over there? He barks every time a ball lands in the rough near their house."
"Why isn't he barking now?"
"After a while he gets hoarse."

Difference between a soft iron shot and a hard iron shot: A soft iron shot makes fewer ripples.

"You want to try to play within yourself," a golf pro said to a golfer.
"Exactly what does that mean?" the golfer asked.
"It means you shouldn't try to play better than you actually are," the golf pro explained.
The golfer thought for a moment. "I think I'm already doing that," he answered.

You can have a lot of laughs discussing a golf game, especially when it's someone else's golf game.

Why is it, when someone says, "Whatever you do, don't hit your ball into the rough on the right," we have to hit our ball into the rough on the right.

Many a golf ball has gone into the left rough because we adjusted our swing to keep it from going into the right rough.

After listening to the description of a game that had been played the previous Saturday, one golfer said to another, "You know, that is just about the best round of golf I have ever heard you fabricate."

"How many strokes did your wife record on that hole?" a husband was asked.
"About two thirds of them," he replied.

A golfer who had gone into a dense thicket of shrubbery after a ball was howling each time he touched a thorny branch.
"Why don't you just leave your ball in there?" another golfer suggested.
"I found my ball two minutes ago," the golfer replied.
"Then why don't you come out?" the other golfer yelled.
"I don't come into a place like this for just one golf ball," the golfer in the thicket yelled back.

"Can I go golfing today?" a husband asked his wife. "All the other husbands are going."
"You're beginning to sound more like the kids every day," she replied.

First wife: "Does your husband have an inflated ego when he's playing golf?"
Second wife: "No. His ego is usually deflated when he's playing golf. It doesn't inflate again until afterwards."

"When I have difficulty falling asleep, I count sheep, and I fall asleep in a few minutes."
"When I have difficulty falling asleep, I count golf shots."
"Really? And how long does it take you to fall asleep?"
"It depends on how long the game takes."

"How are you doing?" a golfer was asked.
"Not bad," he replied.
"Hitting the fairways?"
"Pretty much."
"When was the last time you missed one?"
"Last fairway."

"I'm looking forward to an exciting round of golf today."
"You're in luck. My brother-in-law is playing today, and he'll provide you with lots of excitement. He hits the ball more than 400 yards."
"Oh! Is your brother-in-law in my foursome?"
"No. He's in the foursome behind you."

"All I want is to shoot par or better," a first time golfer exclaimed. "Is that too much to expect?"

Golf pro: "I'm not too happy with your golf game."
Golfer: "*You're* not too happy???!!!"

A husband had been giving his wife lessons.
"How are we doing in our golf game?" he asked.
"Fine," she answered.
"Are we hitting the ball straight?"
"Reasonably."
"How is our putting?"
"Not bad."
"Are you still hitting your drives into the lake?"
"Oh yeah, now it's *my* game."

"My wife and I share the load when we're playing golf. I carry our golf bags, and she opens the trunk of the car."

One golfer was listening to another golfer describe his game. When he had finished, the listener said, "Say, that's really good. Do you mind if I use it in *my* next description?"

"Are you hitting many roughs today?" a golfer was asked.
"Ah," he sighed, "if only I could be that accurate."

"How bad was my golf game today. I'll tell you how bad my golf game was today. On one hole, I forgot how many strokes I had . . . and I was still on the tee."

"Did you hit many greens today?"
"Just one."
"Were you excited?"
"No, but the golfers who were using the practice green were."

Why is it, all the other golfers decide to watch us just as we're about to flub one.

It took me twenty years to discover I couldn't golf worth a darn, but by then I was enjoying myself so much I couldn't quit.

"What is your goal?" a golfer who was preparing to tee off was asked.
"To shoot par," he said.
"Would that be on a par seventy course or on a par seventy-two course?" he was asked.
"On one hole," he answered.

A golfer arrived home, grumbling to himself after shooting a disastrous round. He was surprised when his wife asked him to describe how his game went.
"Why?" he exclaimed.
"One of your friends called," she replied. "He said you had finally shot a game I would enjoy hearing about."

Practice green: Every one of them.

One golfer hit so many golf balls into the rough, his caddy came with a search party.

Just when you think you are finally getting the hang of golf, along comes a high shot into a stiff wind.

Golfers know *how* to hit every shot in the game, but darned if they *can* hit them.

"How did you become such a good golfer?"
"I've *divotted* my life to it."

"I think you're a crappy golfer."
"You're not really certain, are you?"

One foursome was so slow that the manager of the golf course came by and told them to get back to work.

"I don't boast a lot about my golf game."
"You have a lot not to boast about."

"Is it true," a person unfamiliar with the game inquired of a golfer, "that in the game of golf a low score is the sign of a good game?"
"Not with the golfers I play with," the golfer replied.

A professional golfer had a one night fling. When it was over, the woman he had the affair with said, "I was just thinking."
"Thinking about what?" the golfer asked.
"Thinking about what we should do if I become pregnant," she responded.
The golfer closed his eyes.
"What are you doing?" she asked.
"Praying," he said.
"Praying for what?" she asked.
"A mulligan," he replied.

"This is one of my two favorite golf courses," an old timer informed a couple of younger players, "but they tend to keep the other course in better playing condition come fall."
Thinking they might try the other golf course themselves, one of the younger players asked, "Where is this other course?"
"Florida," the old timer replied.

"I shot a 75 today. I had been shooting a 94, but then I was in the rough, and my ball was buried, and another golfer said that under winter rules I could improve my lie. That's when I decided to shoot a 75."

A golfer sliced five straight drives into a lake. "Why did you hit so many, when you knew they were going to go into the lake?" another golfer asked.
The golfer shrugged. "For the first hundred yards they looked O.K."

Golfers have three scores. The score they give themselves, the score they give everyone else, and the score everyone else gives them.

"Do you have any tee times?" a golfer asked a clerk in the pro shop. "I told my wife that I would mow the grass right after I finished my golf game."
"We can get you on right away," the clerk informed him.
"Don't you have something a little later in the day?" the golfer replied.

"Would you show me how to hit a golf ball?" a wife asked her husband.
"Sure," he replied, then he drove his ball into a lake.
"I already know how to do that," she said.

A golfer happened to be placed in a foursome that included a woman who was raising funds for a local charity. During the round their conversation turned to the used articles sale her group was holding the following week.
"You wouldn't happen to have an old set of golf clubs you would like to get rid of?" she inquired.
"As a matter of fact I do," the golfer answered.
"Would you care to donate them to our fund drive?" she asked.
"I'm sorry, I can't," the golfer replied.
"Why not?" she asked.
"Because I'm playing with them," he answered.

The difference between an experienced golfer and a beginner: A beginner worries about his ball going into the lake, and consequently that's where it goes. An experienced golfer ignores the lake and sees only the fairway. His ball still goes into the lake, but he figures it was worth a shot.

"I hate playing golf with younger people," a husband complained. "They hit the ball longer, they hit the ball straighter, they putt better, they're full of confidence, they're cocky, they tell me how to play . . . ."
"Does this mean you're not taking the kids with you any more?" his wife asked.

"What would you say if I told you all my drives are hitting the fairway?" a golfer said.
"I would say your drives aren't going far enough," another golfer replied.

"What causes me to hit my golf ball into a lake?" a student asked a golf pro.
"For some reason, golf balls just like to go there," the pro answered.
"Then what causes me to hit my golf ball into the rough?" the student asked.
"For some reason, golf balls like to go there too," the pro said.
"What if my golf ball could make a choice between going into the rough or a lake?" the student asked.
"Your golf ball would never go into the rough if it has a lake to go into," the pro replied.

"Have you noticed that children's books contain a lot of pictures to help them understand the story?" a wife asked her husband.

"Yes," he answered.

"And have you noticed that adult books don't require a lot of pictures to help them understand the story?" she asked.

"Yes," he answered. "So what's your point?"

"Nothing," she replied. "I was just wondering if there's some significance to golf instruction books having so many pictures."

"My husband likes to play with younger golfers."

"Oh? Do they help him keep his game sharp?"

"No. They help him see where his ball goes."

A robber went into a pro shop and said to the clerk, "Stick 'em up, give me your valuables, and while you're at it, give me money for a tee time."

The clerk replied, "We don't carry that much cash."

Where else can you find a game, where the more difficult it becomes, the more people want to play.

"How bad was my golf game today? I'll tell you how bad my golf game was today. My golf game was so bad today, I didn't feel comfortable with my second shot unless I was lining it up through tree branches."

Learning the swing is one of the easiest lessons in golf. I've managed to learn hundreds of them.

A pollster asked golfers if they had ever lied about their score.
50 percent said they had, and 50 percent said they hadn't.
When the poll was published, it read, "50 percent of golfers tell truth about lying. Other 50 percent continue to lie."

One golfer commenting on another golfer's game: "He shaves more strokes than our neighborhood barber."

"Everything I know about golf, I taught myself."
"It's nice to see you're man enough to take the blame."

"Do you have any tee times open?"
"Sorry, we don't have any tee times open. We also have an emergency. One of our golfers fainted on the first tee and had to be taken to the hospital."
"Then you do have a tee time open . . . ."

"No matter how badly I play golf, I still like it more than working."
"You must have hated work a lot."

"I've already forgotten about the poor round I had yesterday. I don't believe in playing golf in the past."
"If I had your game, I wouldn't be too thrilled about playing it in the future either."

The way I see it, a hook is just a slice that doesn't know where it's going.

I went to a golf pro who advertised himself as a specialist.
I asked, "What makes you a specialist?"
He answered, "I only teach the five iron."

Into every life some rain must fall. Some seems to fall every time I make a tee time.

Two little boys were talking.
One says, "How come your parents named you Chipper?"
The other answers, "Because my father was golfing when my mother went into labor, and he happened to be using his chipper at the time."
"Wow," the first exclaimed. "What an interesting way to get your name, Chipper."
"If you think my name is interesting," Chipper replied, "wait until you meet my brothers and sisters, Putter, Driver, Sand Wedge, and Three Iron."

"Are you a good golfer?"
"I'm an excellent golfer. Who wants to know?"
"My wife."
"Why?"
"You're standing in her garden."

If you need proof that golf is more popular than work, just ask yourself, "When was the last time you gave someone a day's pay to let you work?"

"When did you decide to marry your wife?" one husband asked another.
"When we were dating," the other husband replied, "and she said to me, what did you do today? And I said, I went golfing. And she said, oh, tell me about it."

"How was your husband's golf game today?"
"Not very good. Some of his drives were so short, he was able to describe them with hand gestures."

"Do you believe in a lucky bounce?" a golfer in the fairway asked a golfer in the rough.
"Does it look like I believe in a lucky bounce?" the golfer in the rough replied.

"I have never golfed before," one husband told another. "I just started golfing because my wife started."
"That's nice that you both enjoy golf."
"I hate golf."
"Then why are you playing?"
"I thought I had better learn something about the game if I was going to tell her how to play."

After watching a member of their foursome whack away for several minutes at a ball that was buried deep in the rough, one of the golfers asked, "How's he doing?"
To which another answered, "Not very good, although I think he might be getting closer to the green. He's switched to a higher numbered club."

The two best ways to KEEP other golfers happy:
1/ KEEP up to the group ahead.
2/ KEEP ahead of the group behind.

"What is the difference between a man golfer and a woman golfer?" a teenager asked her mother.
"The main difference is what they see when they look down the fairway," the mother replied. "When they tee up their ball for their first drive, a woman sees 150 yards down the middle of the fairway, and a man sees 300 yards down the middle of the fairway."
"And what do they see for their second shot?"
"For their second shot, the woman sees another 150 yards down the middle of the fairway."
"And the man?"
"He usually sees a lot of tall grass and trees."

First golfer: "My wife isn't talking to me, ever since I played that 36 holes of golf and forgot to let her know where I was."
Second golfer: "How long ago did this take place?"
First golfer: "Saturday and Sunday."

A good golfer is a person who can hit the ball the way we *think* we can hit the ball.

"I don't like being paired with golfers who don't know how to play," a grizzly old timer remarked to a beginner.
"And I don't mind at all being paired with golfers who don't know how to play," the beginner replied. "Please go ahead and tee off."

"I was all tensed up, so I decided to come golfing to relax . . . . Why is everybody laughing?"

"Your golf game stinks."
"Well thank you very much."
"For what?"
"For acknowledging that I have a golf game."

"Did you know that when you swing just right, your hands don't hurt and your club hardly makes a sound when it hits the ball?"
"Really? I have never experienced that."

"I heard that your husband got into an argument with a truck driver this morning."
"Yes. They had a disagreement over on the interstate."
"Was it before or after his golf game?"
"During."

"Is that your husband on the practice range?"
"Yes. He's practicing his shots so he'll be ready for the golf season."
"He doesn't appear to be doing very well. His drives are going all over the place."
"Yep, he'll be ready all right."

"I can drive my golf ball out of sight," a golfer said, "but first I need the right atmospheric conditions."
"And what atmospheric conditions would that be?" he was asked.
"Foggy," he replied.

"You just broke a window in that house over there with your golf ball."
"And you said I couldn't hit anything . . . ."

Young golfers see better than they aim. Old golfers aim better than they see. Middle-aged golfers aim and see about the same, which isn't saying much.

"That golfer ahead has a very nice swing."
"Oh? Did you watch him take his drive off the tee?"
"No. I hit my ball a little too soon, and I watched him hit it back to me."

Two little boys were talking.
"My Dad has golfed overseas," one remarked.
"Wow!" the other replied. "And my Mom says that my Dad can't even hit his ball over a lake."

A home owner was getting tired of rodents from a nearby golf course eating the garden he had planted, so he set some traps. He never did catch a rodent, but he did catch three golfers.

THE ORIGIN OF GOLF

Have you ever wondered how the Scots, or whoever came up with the game of golf, came up with the game of golf?

What person in his right mind would design a game where the goal is to hit an object into a hole with a stick? What person in his right mind would come up with a game where the goal is to hit an object into a hole that is so far away that another stick is needed to indicate where the hole is?

Have you ever wondered what the first golf clubs looked like? I believe that's exactly what they were, clubs. After a battle with the English, the Scotsman's weapons were hanging there on the wall, or sitting in the basement, or leaning against the garage, or wherever they kept their clubs in the fourteenth century, and a Scotsman, after being told by his wife to clean up the yard, decided instead to grab his clubs and head for the pasture to hit something, very much like golfers do today when told to clean up the yard.

But hit what? All the Englishmen had gone home. Now I could be wrong here, but I believe the word golf could have originated from Gauls, a fighting clan that the Scots would occasionally do battle with. Maybe that's what the Scotsman was doing, pretending he was taking a swing at the Gauls.

What were the first gauls bauls, or golf balls if you prefer, made of? When I was a kid we played hockey with road apples (frozen horse manure). Maybe that's what the Scots used. Maybe the road apples reminded them of the English (keep in mind that this was right after they had been in a battle with the English). It's obvious they couldn't play with frozen cow patties, no matter how much they reminded them of the English (they wouldn't roll), and frozen sheep pellets would be too small. Does anyone know if golf originated in the winter? It would probably be pretty sloppy in the summer, what with the thawing road apples and all.

Where did the first golf course originate? I would think a pasture that had been grazed down by sheep. The roughs were probably fence corners and the like that the sheep hadn't touched. Sand traps, well they were probably just that, pockets of sand that the owner of the pasture dug for spite to annoy the golfers. Lakes especially could be a problem, what with getting the road apples out before they thawed. Maybe that's where, "Leave it there and take a stroke and a drop," came from.

The greens? They were probably placed in an area where only the finest sheep grazed. The most difficult greens were probably placed over a gopher hole on the side of a hill, from whence the design of many of our present greens came from.

The greatest accomplishment of all in gauls, or golf, was the club house. I can imagine a group of ten or twelve Scotsmen out for a round of pasture horse hockey ball, or gauls, or whatever it was called back then, and they're all out of road apples because they've hit everything they brought with them into a lake or lost them along the fence corner roughs.

"Nuts," one of them probably said. "Now I'm going to have to go home, and I've only played eighteen pastures."

"Just a minute," another one answered. "Didn't we tell our wives that we were going to be gone all day doing whatever it is we're doing here. If we go home early today, they're going to expect us to come home early every day."

"I know what," another said. "Why don't we build ourselves a shelter. We'll tell our wives it's to store our clubs or something. We can call it a club house. And we can sit in it and eat and drink and talk about our game, or whatever it is we're doing."

"They would never believe that story," another said. "I have a better idea. We've played eighteen of these pastures. Why don't we just tell them we're playing the nineteenth pasture, and that's what we'll call it, the nineteenth pasture."

"And we could use the time that we spend in the club house, or nineteenth pasture, to make up stories about how great we are at whatever we're doing here," another said.

And so it was. War was replaced by gauls, or golf. Of course some Scotsmen also believed the word golf was derived from 'gopher' because of the holes in the greens in the sides of the hills. Many golfers still do.

....

England eventually won the war with Scotland because of something an English commander picked up as he watched Scottish marksmen take aim with their bows and arrows.

All their shots were missing fifty yards to the right.

A golfer was asked where golf originated.
"No one knows for sure," he replied.
"I heard it was Scotland."
"They were given credit for it."
"By whom?"
"The English. They used to play the game quite often."
"Why would England give Scotland credit for inventing golf?"
"It was during one of their wars. The English soldiers couldn't bring themselves to hate the Scottish soldiers enough to go into battle against them."
"So?"
"So the English rulers started a rumor that the Scots invented golf."
"And?"
"And after that, they had no trouble at all hating them."

I got tired of making the same old mistakes with my golf game, so I changed my swing. Now I'm working on a whole new set of mistakes.

"One thing about rain, it separates the golfers from the non golfers. Want to go bowling?"

A father took his children golfing with him.
"Daddy says we're just as good as he is," one of them said when they returned home.
"There, there," soothed their mother. "I'm sure you'll improve."

"How was your golf game today?"
"I played with some nice people."
"I didn't play very well either."

A beginner asked, "How many strokes does it take to get a birdie?"
The old timer replied, "It depends on the hole. Sometimes it takes four, sometimes it takes three, and sometimes it takes only two."
The beginner nodded in approval and said, "I like your method."

Trying to help a student describe the level of his game, a golf pro asked, "If you were to compare your game to a meal, would you say it was more like a tenderloin steak, a New York steak, a rib eye steak, or a hamburger?"
The student thought for a moment and then replied, "Probably more like a beef stew."

Before a golfer sliced his ball into the lake, all of the club fit into his bag. After his shot, only part of the club fit into his bag - the part before the right angle.

Two golfers were watching a third.
"He says he's going to complete this hole with an iron shot and a putt," one said.
"That's going to be interesting to watch," the other replied.
"What? To see how close he can get to the hole with his iron shot?"
"No. To see him make a 100 yard putt."

When I asked another golfer to suggest the best way to hit a tough green, he replied, "Pretend it's a lake." After I took my shot he added, "I said lake, not freeway."

"Didn't you hear us yelling at you about how slow we've had to play?" a golfer said to a poky foursome ahead.
"That's O.K.," a member of the foursome replied. "We've been playing kind of slow ourselves."

Two golfers were examining the score card of their playing partner, Charlie.
"I wish I could golf this well," one of the golfers said.
"Charlie wishes he could golf this well," the other golfer answered.

"I took something today that caused my game to drop from over a hundred to just above eighty."
"Wow! What was it?"
"Twenty mulligans."

"These golf clubs have been successfully getting me out of roughs and sand traps for more than fifteen years, but now it's time I got rid of them."
"But if you've been successful with them, why are you getting rid of them?"
"Would you hang on to golf clubs that have been getting you into roughs and sand traps for more than fifteen years?"

An optimist is a golfer on the first tee. A pessimist is a golfer on the eighteenth tee. A realist is a golfer who is about to begin his second round.

"I can't seem to find my swing today," a golfer complained.
"You're lucky," another golfer replied. "I can't seem to lose mine."

A professional golfer was asked what she missed most from her amateur days.
"The mulligan," she replied.

"What kind of golfer is your husband?" a wife was asked.
"All kinds," she replied.

"How is your golf game?"
"It comes and goes, depending . . . ."
"Depending on what? The day? The weather? The course conditions . . . ?"
"The club, the ball, the fairway, the shot . . . ."

"Where did you learn such atrocious language?" a dignified lady demanded of a golfer who was cussing and flailing away in the rough.
"I don't know," the golfer answered. "It just seems to show up every time my ball lands here."

"I prayed last night."
"What did you pray for?"
"A better golf game."
"What did you say?"
"I said, God, I have a serious problem with my golf game."
"And what did God say?"
"He said, I know you have a serious problem with your golf game."
"What did he say after that?"
"Nothing."
"Nothing . . . ????"
"Nothing . . . except . . . ."
"Except what?"
"I think I might have heard some laughter."

A young boy, who had accompanied his father to the golf course, watched as one after another the other golfers drove their balls into the rough. Finally he turned to his father and said, "Do you think we should tell them they're supposed to be aiming for that hole with the stick in it?"

After they putt out, why do some golfers feel the only place suitable to fill out a score card is in the middle of the green.

A young man, who had just taken up golf, was enthusiastically telling others how much he was enjoying himself.
"To think that my father has been playing golf for all of my life, and I never went with him," he exclaimed.
"Why did you never go?" he was asked.
"Listening to him, I didn't think it was any fun," he answered.

One golfer liked to conceal his skills so that no one could steal them. He did a good job at it. No one has seen any for twenty years.

"My wife hit fifty percent of the greens this morning . . . and that was before she left the first tee."

"That's a unique swing," one golfer said to another. "Did it cost a lot to learn it?"
"Five thousand dollars," was the reply.
"That's a lot of money just to learn a swing."
"Oh, it only cost two hundred dollars to learn the swing," the unique golfer responded. "The other forty-eight hundred was for the physiotherapist."

"I just found four golf balls in my yard," an angry home owner said to a golfer who was searching for his ball.
"They can't be mine," the golfer answered. "I only hit three."

"How many months in your golf season?" a new golfer asked the club pro.
"Six," the pro replied, "except for the really dedicated golfers. They usually play an extra three months in the spring and three months in the fall."

A golfer had tried to get a tee time at just about every course in the city, without any luck. Desperate to play, he finally settled for a small rundown course.
"Kinda short, isn't it?" he said to the clerk as he examined the yardage on the score card.
"Yep," the clerk replied, taking his money.
When the golfer had finished his round, he went into the club house again. "This course is in the worst condition I've ever had to play on," he complained.
"Kinda makes you happy that it's so short, doesn't it," the clerk replied.

"I've heard that men consider their golf game to be an extension of their sexuality," one wife said to another.
"I sure feel sorry for their sexuality," the other wife replied.

Golf looks easy on paper. If you don't believe me, just read a few score cards.

I was playing really poor golf and thought I had lost my swing, so I returned to my golf instructor for some lessons.
"No, you have not lost your swing," he said.
I was feeling much better, until he added, "I'm afraid this is the same swing you've always had."

One golfer only uses clubs made in Japan. He thinks they drive better.

"Which hole on this course do you think has the easiest green to hit?"
"Probably this one."
"What makes you say that?"
"I missed all the others."

A husband noticed that his wife had attached some notes to her clubs. One note said, "Slices," another said, "Hooks," and another said, "Hits reasonably straight."
"Why doesn't this one have a note?" he asked, pulling out a club.
"It can't seem to make up its mind," she answered. "It's still going all over the place."

"Which costs more," a golfer was asked, "golf equipment or the golf itself?"
"I used to think golf equipment," the golfer answered. "Of course that was before I paid for my first tee time."

"The more things change, the more they remain the same."
"That's pretty well sums up my golf game, except for the remaining the same part."

"I've heard that once you develop a slice, it's difficult to get rid of."
"That's true. It happened to me."
"Really? When did you develop your slice?"
"My first shot."

"Have you ever asked your wife to go golfing with you?" a golfer was asked.
"Yes," he replied, "but I don't think she wants to be a golfer. I think she prefers just being a mother and a housewife."
"What makes you say that?"
"Well, the other day she asked me what I would like for my birthday, and I said a sleeve of golf balls."
"So, how does that prove she doesn't want to be a golfer?"
"She's in the other room knitting a sleeve."

"Where did you get the black eye?"
"I was swinging through the ball just a little too early."
"How could swinging through the ball early give you a black eye?"
"My swing was O.K. It was the golfer who was still in the fairway when I took it that gave me the black eye."

"I'm certainly not the golfer I used to be," a golfer complained.
"Thank heaven for that," another player in his foursome responded.

A manufacturer designed a set of clubs for golfers with low self esteem. When you hit a poor shot, they take the blame.

After hitting their first drives, two golfers lost sight of each other until they met at the green.
"How did you make out?" one of them asked.
"Well," answered the other, "my first drive with my one wood went into the rough on the right side. Then I hit a five iron that went into a sand trap on the other side. My third shot was with a seven iron that rolled into the lake. My fourth shot was with a nine iron that went into the rough on the other side again. Then I hit two pitching wedges and a sand wedge that got me to the green. How did you make out?"
"I just hit one three wood," the second golfer said. "It went straight down the fairway and rolled up to the green."
"I suppose that's another way I could have done it," the first golfer replied.

"Here today, gone tomorrow," a golfer sighed.
"Were you philosophizing about life?" someone asked.
"No," the golfer replied. "Just my swing."

I love golf. It's playing the game that drives me crazy.

"I believe the problem with your swing could be at the end of your arms," a young golfer was told.
"You mean my hands?" he said.
"The other end of your arms, my boy, the other end."

Two golfers found themselves in some deep rough, many yards from the fairway.
"Where is the green, in relation to where we are?" asked one.
"Green!" the other answered. "Green! I'm not looking for the green anymore. I'll be happy if I can just find my way back to the golf course!"

Two golfers were preparing to tee off on the first hole.
"They tell me that one golfer was so frustrated with his game yesterday," the first golfer said, "that he threw his clubs into a lake and vowed he'd never play again."
"I know," the other golfer sheepishly replied. "That was me."

90 Degree Rule: Meant for drivers of electric golf carts to stay on the cart path and then turn toward the center of the fairway so as to save the grass. More generally used by golfers hitting their shots off the tee - their drives go down the center of the fairway and then turn toward the cart path.

A golfer had taken six unsuccessful swings, trying to get his ball out of the rough. When his seventh swing finally connected and sent the ball flying into a nearby lake, he remarked, "I thought I was never going to get out of that grass."

A golfer is a person who can carry fifty pounds of golf equipment for four miles, but can't find the strength to get off the sofa to change the T.V. channel.

Golf is a lot like going to a comedy revue. In comedy, a group of people watch a comedian tell a joke, and then they laugh. In golf, a group of people watch a golfer take a swing at his ball, and then they laugh. The only difference is, in comedy, they can let the comedian know.

"Are you still dreaming about getting a hole in one?" one golfer asked another.
"No," the other golfer replied. "Now I'm happy if I can just hit a fairway in one."

"Have you ever prayed during a golf game?"
"Once, when I took twelve shots to play a par three hole."
"Did you get an answer?"
"Yep."
"What did he say?"
"He said, if you think this hole's bad, wait 'till you get to the water on number sixteen."

"Are you a good golfer?" a golfer was asked.
"No, and I'm glad I'm not," he replied.
"Why is that?" he was asked.
"Because if I were any good, I'd be tempted to play more," he said.

"This is the worst golf course I've ever played on," a golfer complained to a golf pro.
"Why, thank you," the golf pro replied. "I knew when I saw you take your first swing that you and our course would have a lot in common."

GOLF MEANINGS

A little too much fade: You're in the lake again.

A little too much draw: You're in the lake on the other side.

A bad day golfing is still better than a good day working: You're either having a bad day golfing or you're working.

Concentrate on the ball: And maybe you'll hit it.

I should have used a seven: You could have used a bazooka, and you still would have missed the green.

I didn't feel like golf today anyway: You forgot to make a tee time again.

I was hitting them O.K. at practice: Yes, but then the driving range is two hundred yards wide.

Nice putt: Your ball is still on the green.

We really enjoyed having you play golf with us today: You brought us a lot of laughter.

You sure caught a piece of that one: If you had caught the entire ball, it might still be in the fairway.

I'm getting more distance: Your drives are going farther into the rough.

You got good height on that one: 200 yards, straight up.

Your game's getting better: It couldn't possibly get any worse.

It doesn't look like my ball: It really is your ball, but since it bounced off his house, and he's looking for the ball's owner . . . .

I shot my age today: You don't look 110.

Perhaps if you slowed your swing down a little: And maybe you'll hit the ball.

Perhaps if you speed your swing up a little: We've been out here five hours and would like to go home sometime today.

Longest drive you've had today: You hit it past the end of the tee box.

Stupid place to put a lake: You know where his ball went.

Rough: A golfer's language after a bad shot.

Looks like a nice day to play golf: You're cleaning up the back yard again.

Utility club: The bar beside the pro shop after a tough game.

This can't be your ball: You finally hit one that landed in a fairway.

Nineteenth hole: The only good hole on the course.

Someone coughed: Or laughed.

The back nine: The part of the course where we try to figure out what went wrong on the front nine.

It's not whether you win or lose at golf, it's how you play the game: It's whether you win or lose.

That one looks like it's going straight: Yeah, straight toward the highway.

REASONS FOR DRIVING POORLY

I need new clubs.

I just got new clubs.

I need new grips.

I just got new grips.

If only I'd used a longer club.

If only I'd used a shorter club.

If only it had gone straight.

If only it hadn't rained.

I didn't have a chance to practice this week.

The air's too heavy.

I didn't know that lake was there.

Stupid ball.

Stupid club.

Stupid game.

REASONS FOR PUTTING POORLY

There was a shadow over the hole.

I didn't see that spike mark.

Is there a break there???

Green's too fast.

Green's too slow.

My putter needs regripped.

Just had my putter regripped.

Don't stand there.

You moved.

I need a new putter.

Where's my old putter.

They were going in at practice.

Stupid cup location.

Stupid game.

**"Every time I play golf, I can't help but think about my job."
"What do you think about it?"
"I think I'd rather not have it."**

Sign in club house: Lost - five iron. Last seen leaving the fourteenth fairway.

**"That foursome that is getting ready to tee off consists of one golfer and three duffers," one golfer informed another.
"How can you tell?" the other golfer inquired.
"Because they told me," the first golfer said.
"Which one said he was the golfer?" the other golfer asked.
"All of them," the first golfer replied.**

And then there was the student who thought he would get a better golf score if he was nice to the instructor.

Some golfers have absolutely no confidence. They separate their best golf balls from their water balls, and then they use the water balls.

"My two best shots today were the hook and the slice," one golfer informed another.
"But those are two of the worst shots you can make in golf," the other golfer replied.
The first golfer nodded. "That should give you some idea of what the rest of my game was like."

"They say that a draw goes farther than a fade. I wouldn't know, since my fades and draws are usually 100 yards apart."

"How many shots to make the green on this hole?" a golfer asked as he stared down the fairway at a 535 yard, par five hole.
"Two," the golfer with him said nonchalantly.
The first golfer looked at him incredulously. "What makes you so sure you can make it in two shots?" he asked.
"Because if I don't make it with my first two shots," the confident golfer replied, "I'll surely make it with the second two."

"If I were to decide to write a book of golf humor, where would I begin?"
"The first tee on any golf course."

Why is it: The same sun that makes it too hot for us to work in the back yard isn't too hot to keep us off the golf course.

"Just play your own game," a golf pro advised an erratic golfer.
"That's what I've been doing," the golfer answered. "Now, if you don't mind, I'd like to try someone else's game."

Why is it? Golfers can't remember their high scores, and won't let us forget their low scores.

"If after you finish your lessons," a golf pro said to a student, "you were to play golf, and the person you were playing with shot par on every hole, and you shot four over par on every hole, what would the difference be?"
"The main difference," the student replied, "would be my new golf instructor."

The difference between a golf score and the weather: You can't improve the weather with a pencil.

"Golf balls are becoming just too expensive. Yesterday a golfer asked me if I would help him find one that he lost in the rough."
"So, how does that make them expensive?"
"He offered me a reward."

"I have some good news for you," a golf instructor informed his students, "and some bad news."
"What's the bad news?" one of the students asked.
"None of you can hit the ball straight," the instructor said.
"And what's the good news?" a student asked.
The instructor smiled. "No one else can either."

A young golfer who went into a pro shop to get a tee time was mistaken for an applicant who was supposed to come in for a job interview.
The first question he was asked was, "Can you start at three-thirty in the morning?"
"I suppose, if I have to," he answered.
"And do you mind if you don't finish until late in the day?"
"You sure must have a lot of slow players here," the young golfer said.

"How did you do that?" one golfer asked another whose drive had gone 275 yards straight down the middle of the fairway.
"I don't know," the golfer who had made the drive answered, "but it's sure going to slow my game down."
"How can a 275 yard drive straight down the middle of the fairway possibly slow your game down?" the other golfer asked.
"Because I'm going to stand over it and admire it for a while," the successful golfer replied.

A golfer was at a business meeting when another man he didn't know walked into the room.
"See that fellow who just came in," an associate whispered to him. "He's one of the most dishonest, lying, cheating, conniving people I know."
"Really?" the golfer replied. "What course does he play on?"

Seeing no one on the fairway, a foursome hit their first drives. They were about to start out to find their golf balls and take their second shots when they noticed the foursome ahead, in the rough, looking for their first drives.

I used to worry about reaching my level of incompetence, but not anymore. I reach it just about every time I golf.

After another drive that went deep into the rough, a golfer was heard to mutter, "I'll hit my *$@#%*&$ golf ball anywhere I *$@#%*&$ well please!"

"What is the longest distance you ever hit a ball?" a golf instructor inquired.
"200 yards," a student responded.
"And the least yards?"
"Zero," the student replied.

"I'm thinking about writing a book about my golfing experiences and all the skills I have acquired."
"Oh, a fantasy."

A good golf swing is just a matter of timing. You have to time your swing so that the club head goes through the ball just a moment before, or just a moment after, you actually do it.

"Let's say," said the golf instructor, "that you and another golfer have both driven your golf balls deep into the rough, and that when you get to them, one of the balls is sitting nicely up on the grass while the other is buried, but you can't see the markings on either ball to tell which belongs to you and which belongs to the other golfer. What would you do?"
"I'd hit the ball that's sitting up," the student replied, "unless of course, the other golfer gets there first."

I used to be awfully disappointed in how few yards my ball went. So I began measuring my drives in feet. Now I feel much better about my distance. I'm also shooting lower scores on the par twelves.

Course manager: "Did you make that SLOW, GOLFERS CROSSING sign and instal it out on the street like I asked?"
Assistant: "Yes, but I have to do it again. I printed it wrong."
Course manager: "How come?"
Assistant: "I didn't know it was supposed to have a comma."

Not all golfers have the same abilities. Some are able to drive their ball much farther into the rough than others.

"A day without golf is like a day without . . . ."
"A day without sunshine?"
"I was going to say aggravation."

"My husband made a decision to cancel his golf game today because he didn't think he would play very well."
"How could he possibly make a decision that he wouldn't play well before he even played?"
"He didn't make the decision before he played. He made it while in a foot of rough beside the fifth fairway."

"What is the main difference between golfing and bowling?"
"Well, first there is the ball . . . ."

You know you haven't had a good golf game when the most pleasurable part you can remember is the walk to the first tee.

Two little girls were watching as the mother of one sorted through some golfing equipment. Eventually the mother stopped at a bag, pulled out a seven iron, and said, "This one should be suitable."
"What's she doing?" asked one.
"Picking out a golf club for my father," said the other.
"Does she always pick out golf clubs for him?" asked the first.
"Only when he comes home late," the other little girl answered.

A bowler was cussing angrily after throwing a ball that landed in the gutter.
"If that's what bowling does to a man when he misses a shot," a bystander commented, "I'm going to take up golf."

A small city had four golf courses. Three of them had erected signs claiming to be the longest. A cynical golfer telephoned the fourth and asked if their course also claimed to be the longest.
The clerk said, "Nope. Can't say that it is. But it sure seems that way."
The golfer made a tee time.

A golfer was inspecting different lines of golf equipment in the pro shop.
"What is this club called?" he inquired, examining a driver.
"It depends," answered the sales clerk.
"On what?" the golfer asked.
"On where your ball lands," the clerk replied.

While playing in the higher elevations of the mountains, a golfer was informed that he could expect to add at least ten percent distance to his drives in the thinner air.
"Do you know what that means for the drive you just made?" another golfer asked.
"Yes," he replied. "It means it went another twenty yards into the lake."

"Great, fantastic, best game I've had all year!" a golfer was heard exclaiming to himself as he walked off the eighteenth green.
"What do you mean, great, fantastic, best game you've had all year?" another golfer said. "That was the worst golf you ever played."
"I know," the first golfer replied. "I'm just practicing in case someone *asks* me *how* I played."

First golf pro: "I'm giving up golf instruction."
Second golf pro: "Why?"
First golf pro: "My students ask too many difficult questions."
Second golf pro: "Such as . . . ?"
First golf pro: "Such as . . . how do I hit the ball straight . . . ?"

"My husband is watching T.V. in preparation for his golf game on Saturday," one wife said to another.
"What's he watching?" the other wife asked. "The golf channel?"
"No," the first wife replied. "The weather channel."

"My wife says she married me because I made her laugh."
"If she laughs that easily, you'd better not take her golfing."
"Where do you think we met."

"You know, you're really quite a good golfer," a beginner was told.
"It came as a surprise to me too," she replied.

"You didn't count your strokes for the two balls you hit into the lake," a husband informed his wife.
"And I'm not going to count them," his wife replied.
"Why not?" he asked.
"Because I left them there," she said.

"My doctor moonlights as a golf instructor. I said I was having problems with my swing. He told me to hit two buckets of balls and call him in the morning."

"See that golfer over there. He's so bad, he once hit five shots in a row into a lake."
"I'm sure there must be other golfers who have done that."
"Not before they left the putting green."

A golfer had been forced to spend a few days in bed because of illness.
"I'm sorry you won't be playing Saturday," one of his buddies sympathized.
"I might be sick," the golfer replied, "but I'm not that sick."

"How often do you hit a golf ball into a lake?" a golfer was asked.
"It depends on the lake," he answered.
"Why is that?" he was asked.
"If it's really deep with steep sides, I only hit it in once," he replied.

You might assume your date isn't exactly enjoying her first day golfing, if halfway down the third fairway she says, "I'm sorry, I have to leave, I have another appointment."

"When did you stop laughing at other golfers?" a golfer was asked.
"When I became one," he answered.

A golfer telephoned a golf course he was not familiar with to get a tee time. The clerk who answered the phone was extremely busy.
"How long does it take to play your course?" the golfer asked when the clerk answered.
"Just one moment," the clerk said as he switched lines and went to a previous caller.
"Thank you," the golfer said, "but I was looking for something a little longer."

"I help my wife when she's golfing."
"Oh? How do you do that?"
"I warn the other golfers that she's getting ready to take her shot."

"I don't think my husband is very serious about helping me with my golf swing," one wife said to another. "I asked him, how do I hit a golf ball straight down the fairway? He answered, just keep swinging. You'll come to it eventually."

"I can tell how a golfer is doing just by watching his body language as he swings through the ball," a golf pro said to a golfer's wife.
"I can tell how my husband is doing just by listening to his body language," the wife answered.

"I wonder how your drive ended up on the green?" one golfer said to another who was getting ready to putt. "The last time I saw your ball, it was heading toward the middle of that lake over there."
"The other golfer thought for a moment, and then replied, "Lucky bounce . . . ?"

"Are you a good golfer?"
"Yes."
"But your ball is in the lake."
"What do I know."

"What distance does a golf ball have to be from the hole before it's considered a gimme?"
"Twelve inches."
"So, anything less than twelve inches is a gimme?"
"No. Anything more than twelve inches is a gimme. If it's less than twelve inches, we figure we can make it, so we putt out."

I'm hoping they'll get rid of the present scoring system in golf and put in a grading system like they use in college. As long as they grade on the curve, it should help my game.

A beginner had been trying to hit her golf ball off the practice tee for several minutes. Each time she swung, she missed. Finally, her club grazed the top of the ball, sending it five feet.
"See," her instructor exclaimed. "Didn't I say you were a natural."

"I don't think my golf game is what it used to be, but on the other hand, I don't think it ever was what I thought it used to be."

"Have you ever shot your age in golf?"
"Yes, just this morning."
"Really?"
"Yes. Once on the front nine, and once again on the back nine."

I was very pleased the first time I played golf, breaking par half way through the first hole and all, then I learned you break par with your score going in the other direction.

"Which hole on this course do you consider the most valuable?" a golfer asked a club pro.
"That one over there," the pro said.
"What do you mean, that one over there?" the golfer exclaimed. "That's a lake."
"I know," the pro answered.
"So how can that be the most valuable?" the golfer asked.
"It's where we get our range balls," the pro replied.

"I didn't like the look of that last shot," a golfer said as his ball disappeared into a lake.
"Fortunately, you didn't have to look at it long," another golfer commented.

Successful golfers are not afraid to take chances. Golf is a lot like life.

"I've probably learned at least 20 different golf swings over the years," one golfer said to another.
"Really?" the second golfer replied. "And which swing did you bring with you today?"
The first golfer thought for a moment and then answered, "I think I brought them all."

A college student who was trying out for the golf team asked the book store clerk if they had *Cliffs Notes* because he didn't want to practice.

"This golf instruction book is guaranteed to lower your score by 12 strokes," a golfer was told.
"In that case," he replied, "give me three."

Have you noticed, most professional golfers are gracious winners, and they are just as gracious when they don't win.

"That golfer has one of the highest scores ever recorded on this golf course."
"Is he that much worse than everybody else?"
"No. Just more honest than everybody else."

"Do you think golf is an easier game to learn when you're young?" an elderly gentleman was asked.
"Most definitely," he replied. "I think we should all begin before sixty, or at least as soon as we retire."

"This land used to be a race track," one golfer informed another, "until the owner turned it into a golf course."
"So who cares," the other golfer exclaimed. "That doesn't have anything to do with our game. By the way, what's the distance to the green on this hole?"
"Two and a half furlongs," the first golfer replied.

"Which club would you suggest I use here?" a wife asked her husband.
"I told you which club to use on the last hole," he answered, "and you hit your ball into the lake."
"Well, we've passed the lake," his wife replied. "Maybe it will work now."

"Are your golf lessons guaranteed to teach me the game?" a student asked.
"Sure are," the instructor answered. "Do you see that teenager over there?"
"Yes."
"Well, he never golfed before in his life, and after only two minutes of my lessons, he had already learned so much that he was telling me how to play."

"How long do you think it will be until I master the game?" a student asked his instructor.
"I don't know," the instructor replied. "No one has ever lived that long."

A golfer developed amnesia. His memory came back once, but the first thing he remembered was his score, so he decided to keep the amnesia.

Weather Forecast: Heavy rain all day, no chance of clearing until midnight.
What a golfer hears: Slight chance of rain, clearing by noon.

A young reporter played golf with some older newsmen who did not hesitate to take a mulligan or kick a ball out of the rough. Later, he sat in the club house and listened to them brag about the low scores they had shot.
"Well," one of the older reporters inquired, "did you learn anything today?"
"I sure did," the young man replied.
"What?" he was asked.
"I learned that the pen is mightier than more things than just the sword," he responded.

Two heads are better than one in golf, unless of course, one of the heads can't read a green.

"I have some good news and some bad news," one golfer said to another. "The bad news is that somewhere during our game we got lost and missed playing four holes. The good news is we knocked sixteen strokes off our scores."

My wife always enjoys getting out for a game of golf, and the game of golf always enjoys having her.

"I can either take my game to the golf course and watch it fall apart," a golfer muttered, "or I can keep it at home and watch it rot there."

"I gave up golf because of my game," an ex-golfer said. "I didn't have one."

"If you make a hole in one on the seventh hole during this tournament," one golfer said to another, "they give you a new Ford car."
"Nuts," the second golfer answered. "And me a Chevy man."

First golfer: "How was your game?"
Second golfer: "Not very good. I lost four golf balls in the rough and three in the lake."
First golfer: "That's a lot of golf balls to lose in one game."
Second golfer: "What one game. That was on the first hole."

"I could tell by watching your first swing, that with practice you're going to be a very good golfer," an old timer said to a beginner.
"How could you tell all that from watching just one swing?" another golfer inquired.
"I didn't have to watch even one swing," the old timer replied. "I believe that everyone who practices is going to be a good golfer."

Difference between a golfer who is dedicated and a golfer who is not dedicated: A dedicated golfer is golfing. A non dedicated golfer is at home raking leaves.

A tennis player and a golfer were arguing.
"Golfers aren't as accurate as tennis players," the tennis player bragged. "You can't even keep your drives in the fairway."
"We could if we had a fifteen foot high fence around it," the golfer answered.

"A salesman for a golf instruction program said he could give me the perfect swing for $600. I told him I would give him the $600 right after he gave me the perfect swing."

"Are you slicing consistently?" a golf instructor asked a student.
"If I were doing anything consistently," the student answered, "I wouldn't be here."

"One nice thing about this course," a golfer said, "is that they mow the grass every three or four months, whether it needs it or not."

"There's nothing like a good round of golf to cheer a person up," one golfer said to another.
"Then why are you so miserable?" the other golfer asked.
The first golfer grimaced. "Because what I played today was nothing like a good round of golf."

Every time I went golfing, my game got worse and worse. So I decided to quit until it improved.

"I could teach a monkey how to hit a golf ball," an arrogant instructor said to a golfer who was not doing very well.
"Self taught, eh," the golfer replied.

Three golfers in a foursome thought the fourth was cheating because all his drives were landing in the fairway.

Why is it: To a laborer, golf is a luxury. To an executive, it's a business expense.

"Am I allowed a total of five strokes to sink my ball on this hole," a beginner asked, "or only three?"
"You're only allowed three," his golfing partner replied.
"Well, there goes my par," the beginner sighed.

"You aren't a very good golfer," a golfer was told.
"Why thank you," the golfer replied with a broad smile.
"For what?"
"Last year I wasn't even a very poor golfer."

On those days when everything has been going wrong, I just close up shop and go golfing. I figure how much worse can it get . . . .

"I hate all sports."
"Then why do you golf?"
"I hate golf the best."

A reverend hit a shot that sliced into the rough, bounced off a tree, rolled back onto the fairway, driddled up to the green, and stopped a foot from the hole.
"How did you do that?" another golfer asked.
"I think that God must have been with me," the reverend replied.
On his first shot on the next hole, the reverend hit a drive that went into the rough, and just kept going.
"Where is God now?" the other golfer asked.
"He's still back on the other hole admiring that great shot we made," the reverend responded.

Golf scores change over a period of time. Some of the biggest changes appear to take place between the eighteenth green and the club house.

"I bought a golf ball that emits a signal to tell me where it is. I can't find it. But it did lead me to three other balls."

A golfer shook his body to loosen up his joints and muscles. He then strode to the back of the tee box, took a couple of practice swings, closed his eyes for a moment to visualized his drive going down the middle of the fairway, and with all the confidence in the world stepped up to his ball and drove it into a lake.
"Why do my drives always seem so much better before I hit them than after I hit them," he sighed.

"For the past five years my husband has cussed his game to high heaven," a wife said, "but he's much better now."
"Has his game improved?"
"No. But his cussing is getting better."

My wife thinks that watching golf on T.V. is boring. This from a woman who enjoys watching the knitting channel.

A man won a lottery worth fifty million dollars. He was asked what he was going to do with it.
"Oh, I don't know," he replied. "Maybe I'll be able to afford to start golfing again."

I hit a lot of fades. Sometimes they fade into the rough, sometimes they fade into a lake, sometimes they fade into the driving range, sometimes they fade across a highway, sometimes they fade . . . .

"I have been attempting to crack the code that my wife uses to keep track of her golf score. I'm not entirely sure, but I think a three on her card equals a five on the hole, a four on her card equals a six on the hole, and a five on her card equals a seven on the hole. Of course there are those times when a three on her card equals an eight on the hole. I didn't say it was an easy code to crack."

A professional golfer was demonstrating various techniques on working the ball, when one of his fades turned into a very bad slice. His ball left the golf course, bounced off a house, careened back onto the fairway, hit a tree, and then rolled onto the green.
"Are you wondering how you did that?" he was asked.
"No," he replied. "I'm wondering what I'm going to do for an encore."

A golfer went to a doctor because, although he was a fairly good player, he was always having temper tantrums, throwing his clubs, and making life miserable for other golfers.
"You have to give me something to help me relax," he pleaded.
The doctor gave him some tranquilizers with a caution that there could be some side affects. A week later he was back.
"Those pills you gave me are no good," he complained.
"Didn't they help you relax?" the doctor asked.
"Yes, but . . . ."
"Are you still having temper tantrums?"
"No, but . . . ."
"Do others enjoy playing with you now?"
"Yes, but . . . ."
"Then what's your problem?"
"I'm so relaxed," the golfer said, "that my drives are going into roughs, into lakes, into sand traps, sometimes I even miss the course completely."
"Didn't I tell you there could be some side effects," the doctor exclaimed.

Stress in golf? What stress? If you hit a golf ball into a lake, what's the most it can cost you, a stroke or two and a lousy golf ball.

"I suppose some of your worst shots are the ones where you don't know where your ball is going," a non golfer said to a golfer.
"Actually no," the golfer replied. "Some of my worst shots are the ones where I do know where my ball is going."

"Which club should I use for this shot?" a wife asked her husband.
"Your three wood," he suggested.
Unfortunately, her swing was a little off and the club head of her three wood went under the ball, popping it almost straight up in the air.
A few holes later, she asked again, "Which club should I use for this shot?"
"Your three wood," he suggested.
"That's what you told me last time," she said, "and look what happened."

"Can you tell me the difference between a good day golfing and a bad day golfing?" a golfer was asked.
"I'm afraid not," the golfer replied.
"Why not?" the questioner pressed.
The golfer grinned. "I've never had a bad day golfing."

"I just realized," one golfer said to another, "that this golf course has fourteen dog legs to the right. I wonder why?"
"It was designed that way on purpose," the other golfer answered. "The owner has a very severe slice."
"Have there been many complaints from other golfers?" the first golfer asked.
"Not a one," the second golfer replied.

I hit my ball fairly and squarely . . . a fairly good slice and squarely into a lake.

A father was about to show his teenage son the proper way to hold a golf club when the son grabbed it like a baseball bat, swung it back and forth twice, and nonchalantly drove the ball 250 yards straight down the middle of the fairway.
"Could you show me how you did that?" the father asked.

"This fairway used to be a farmer's field," a disgruntled golfer who wasn't very happy with playing conditions was informed.
"I thought it still was," he snarled.

"You've been telling us about that same seven under par score for the past two years," one golfer said to another, "and we're beginning to doubt that you ever made that score."
"I know," the other golfer replied. "I had even begun to doubt myself. So I played that very same course last weekend. I wish you could have been there, because darned if I didn't shoot seven under par again."

"Where do you work?" one golfer asked another as they waited to tee off.
"Over at the federal minimum security prison," the other golfer answered.
"Security guard?" the first golfer asked.
"Prisoner," the other golfer replied.

Sign on club house wall: If you should happen to hit a good shot, please try not to admire it too long. You will hold up the other golfers.

"George has just been named golfer of the year," a fellow golfer announced at a golf banquet, "which should give you some idea of how bad the rest of us played."

"Do you have any suggestions that I could use to become a good golfer?" a teenager asked.
"Practice young man, practice," the golf pro responded.
"Don't you have any other suggestions I could use?" the teenager replied.

A husband asked his wife if she would like to go golfing with him.
"I'll give it a try," she said, "but I don't know anything about golf. I've heard that you can get hit by a golf ball."
"Don't worry about it," he assured her. "Hardly anybody ever gets hit by a ball."
So he took her golfing, and half way through the front nine she suddenly ran off the course.
As she disappeared into the parking lot, her husband said to the others in their foursome, "Perhaps I should have explained what a driving range was."

"That man over there sure is egotistical," one golfer said to another. "All he did was talk about the great golf game he played today. I never did get a chance to tell him about the great golf game I played."

"I always thought I'd be good at golf," one golfer grumbled to another, "until I golfed."

I once played golf with a judge from the Olympics. I let him keep score. On one hole he gave me a 5.9.

One golfer had a wicked drive. He could hit a ball 350 yards. No one knew where his drives were going and all the other golfers worried that they might get hit with a ball. Fortunately, his accuracy was so bad that most of his shots landed deep in the rough or a lake. After some practice his aim improved. Now he's hitting the fairways. If you thought the other golfers were worried before, you should see them now.

Two wives were watching a husband who had hit just about everything except a fairway, and was now thrashing away at a ball in the rough. Finally in disgust, he threw his club into the air and it came down and hit him on the head. "He once asked me if I thought he would make a good brain surgeon," one of the wives said. "Thank goodness he chose golf."

A golfer who had problems controlling his temper developed an ulcer and had to see a doctor. After their visit to the medical center his wife was explaining the results to a neighbor.
“The doctor had some bad news for my husband and some good news for me,” she said.
“What’s the bad news he gave your husband?” the neighbor asked.
“He said he can cure his ulcer, but it means he won’t be able to golf for a while.”
“And the good news for you?”
The wife smiled. “He won’t be able to golf for a while.”

If you want to discover the level of your golf game, add what you think of your skills to what everyone else thinks of your skills, and then divide by two. Some golfers should divide by three.

“Are costs for tee times reasonable here, or are they too high?” a golfer asked
“I suppose it depends,” the clerk replied.
“Depends on what?”
“On whether you’re playing the course, or own the course.”

We began to suspect the course wasn't in very good condition when we asked another golfer, "Is your ball in the rough or the fairway?"
And he answered, "I'm not quite sure."

"The difference between playing a great game of golf and playing a mediocre game of golf is often just a matter of a few inches."
"You mean the distance between the fairway and the rough?"
"No. I mean the distance between the golfer's head and his golf club."

When you ask, "How did you golf today?" some golfers can tell you right away. Others have to wait until they fill out their score card.

"What's the matter?" one golf instructor asked another.
"It's that golfer over there," the other instructor answered. "He asked me if I could help him alter his swing a little."
"So what's the problem?"
The instructor shrugged. "He alters it every time he swings, all by himself."

"Tell you what," one golfer said to another as they finished their round, "I won't tell anybody about your game if you don't tell anybody about mine."

"At first I thought I had a five on that hole," one golfer said to another who was keeping their scores, "but then I wondered if I had a four, although it could have really been a three. No, on second thought, I believe it was a four."
Not being sure, the golfer who was keeping score marked him down for a sixteen.

A wife overheard her husband discussing his game with another golfer.
"I had one drive that was 256 yards," he said, "one that was 264, and one that was 286."
When another wife asked what her husband's score was, she said, "I'm not quite sure, it keeps changing, but the last I heard he was shooting a 286."

The ability to be successful in the game of golf is not what makes it so enjoyable. It's the ability to enjoy the game that makes it such a success.

"I remember playing some *pretty good* golf games when I was younger," a grandfather said.
"Did Grampa really play some pretty good golf games when he was younger?" the children asked their Grandmother.
"He didn't actually play the games," their Grandmother said. "He just remembers them."

"What would you recommend to get rid of a slice?" a golfer asked a golf pro.
"Are you sure you have a slice, and not a hook?" the golf pro answered.
"Yes, but what difference does it make?"
"I can get rid of a hook."
"How?"
"By giving you a slice."
"What about a slice?"
"A slice, I just don't know . . . ."

A fanatical golfer was wincing in pain.
"What's wrong?" another golfer asked.
"I was to the doctor yesterday," the fanatic said. "I injured my back and he said I shouldn't golf for a month."
"Then why are you here?"
"I forgot to ask him which month."

"The reason young people are not encouraged to read adult literature," a father said to his children, "is that adults can tell the difference between fact and fiction. Take your mother's golf score card for instance. This hole is fact, this hole is fiction, this hole is fact, this hole is fiction, this hole is . . . ."

"I drove my ball out of sight," a golfer said. "Unfortunately, out of sight was tall grass in the rough, 25 yards from the tee box."

A golfer was bragging about how much distance he was getting.
"Just how far are your drives going?" one of the other golfers in the foursome asked.
"Two hundred and seventy yards," was his reply.
The other golfers were impressed. They watched as he stepped up to his ball and with a mighty swing sliced it far off the fairway.
"That ball didn't go two hundred and seventy yards," one of them scoffed.
"Sure it did," he answered. "It went two hundred yards down the fairway, and seventy yards into the rough. That's two hundred and seventy yards."

**Worst advice I have ever been given by another golfer. "Play your own game."
Have you seen my game???!!!**

A soccer player took up golf. Fortunately, he was able to use some of the same skills, like kicking the ball.

**"Reminds me of a freeway," one golfer said to another as he looked down the fairway.
"How is that?" the other golfer asked.
"Slow golfers ahead, fast golfers behind," the first golfer replied. "I don't know whether to slow down and relax, or pull out and pass."**

Difference between an optimistic golfer and a realistic golfer: An optimistic golfer believes he can conquer the game. A realistic golfer used to be an optimistic golfer.

One way to let other golfers know how good we are is to describe our game to them Another way is to show them. It's just that our game seems so much better when we describe it.

"Ever since I hurt my arm, I've been shooting twenty-five over par," a golfer said.
"And what were you shooting before you hurt your arm?" another golfer inquired.
"Twenty-five over par," the first golfer said.
"If your score is still the same, why are you blaming your arm?" the other golfer asked.
"Because it's the first time I've been able to blame it," the first golfer responded.

A golf professional was asked which golf shot was the easiest to learn.
"The slice," he answered.

"Does your golf course carry liability insurance to cover injuries if someone should get hit by a golf ball?" a golfer asked.
"We certainly do," the golf pro replied.
"What does it cover?"
"Mostly our workers."

"Golfing with Big Louie on the course can be dangerous."
"Why? Did he hit you with a ball?"
"No. I hit him with a ball."

"If you want to see real happiness, just watch my Mom's face when Dad asks if he can go golfing on Saturday morning."
"So it really makes your Mom happy to see your Dad go golfing."
"It sure does. After he goes golfing, she goes shopping."

A golf fanatic was always watching tournaments on T.V. and recording them so that he could view them later. He even had a television set in the bedroom, and with the split screens that many televisions come with, he was sometimes able to watch two games at the same time.
When asked if her husband's habit of watching two golf games at once while in bed had any effect on her rest, his wife remarked, "I get to sleep twice as fast."

"The owners of the course finally came up with a way to increase profits," a clerk informed a group of golfers as he picked up a microphone. Then he said, "Excuse me, I have to announce some tee times. On the first tee is the Harris eightsome, second up is the Burger eightsome, third up is the Smith eightsome . . . ."

One foursome was so bad that even the winner wouldn't announce his score.

Husband: "Statistics show that the average male golfer hits the ball much farther than the average female golfer."
Wife: "Perhaps it's because it's easier to hit a ball sideways than it is to hit it straight ahead."

"I used to be so poor, I couldn't afford to play golf."
"You didn't know when you were well off."

A new employee on the golf course came into the manager's office. "Well, I've finished mowing the grass like you told me to," he said.
"How come it took you so long?" the manager asked.
"Because it was so tall," the employee answered. "Some of it looks like it hasn't been cut in weeks."
Just then the head grounds keeper charged through the doorway and exclaimed, "Who the hell has been mowing the rough on the first three fairways?"

"How would you describe my game today?"
"Magical."
"Magical . . . ?"
"Yes, magical . . . I mean . . . the way you made all those extra strokes disappear."

"I'll never be as good at golf as you are," one golfer admitted to another.
"Why do you think I play with you," the other golfer replied.

"What do you enjoy most about golf?" a golfer was asked.
"Probably the thrill of approaching the last hole of the day," he replied, "and the anticipation of swapping stories about the great shots we made."
"So the eighteenth is your favorite hole?"
"Who said anything about the eighteenth. I'm talking about the nineteenth."

"My caddy didn't remember my game the same way I did, until I questioned him about it."
"What did you ask him?"
"I asked him if he ever wanted to caddy for me again."

My husband's descriptions of his golf games are getting much better. I used to fall asleep right after he said, "Let me tell you about the great golf game I played . . . ." Now I fall asleep right after he says, "Let me tell you . . . ."

"My drives today were landing just below the horizon," a golfer said to his wife.
"Is that how far you were hitting them?"
"No. That's where the lake was."

"Could you suggest a golf course equal to my game?" one golfer asked another.
"I'm afraid not," the other golfer replied. "They all charge for tee times."

"I'm having difficulty getting my ball close to the hole," one golfer announced to another. "In fact, lately I've been having difficulty getting my ball close to the green." After a moment he added, "I'm even having difficulty keeping my ball in the fairway."
"I think you might have just hit on the reason you're having difficulty getting your ball close to the hole," the other golfer replied.

One wife's definition of a five iron:
"What my husband tells me to use to get *my ball* to the green when he thinks *his nine iron* is enough club to get *his ball* to the green."

A golfer, who had come very close to hitting a member of the foursome ahead with a golf ball, apologized.
"I'm very sorry I just missed you," he said. "I'll try to aim straighter next time."

One golfer watched as another golfer in her foursome prepared to hit her first drive of the day. She put her hand to her forehead in the manner of a soothsayer, closed her eyes, and said, "I see her ball going into the rough on the left."
"Wow!" another golfer exclaimed as the ball went exactly where she had predicted. "That was phenomenal. How did you know that?"
"Know what?" the first golfer replied. "All her shots go into the rough on the left."

"Do you ever try to cover up your golfing mistakes?" a golfer was asked.
"No," he replied. "I drown a lot of them."

For some the cup is always half empty. For others the cup is always half full. When one golfer was reminded of all the lakes and roughs she had hit that day, she replied, "Yes, but look at all the ones I missed."

The last time I played golf, I adjusted my swing. I'm just not sure what I adjusted it too.

After they become successful, some people tend to brag about how great they are. Fortunately, golfers don't have to wait that long.

An old timer was trying to enlighten a beginner about the game of golf.
"Almost every day in this country," he said, "a golfer gets a hole in one."
"Boy," the beginner exclaimed. "He must really be good."

If you're winning at the game of golf, it could be that you're playing better than everyone else. Of course it could also be that everyone else is playing worse than you are.

"Is this your ball that just landed in my kitchen?" an irate homeowner asked a golfer.
"Could be," the golfer replied. "I haven't been able to find it anywhere else."

The trick to enjoying a good round of golf is the ability to continually strive for fifty yards more in our drives than we think we are capable of hitting. The ability to accept fifty yards less than we think we are capable of hitting doesn't hurt either.

"Do you know what I like most about this fairway?" one golfer said to another.
"What?"
"The view of the ocean."
"What do you mean, the view of the ocean? The fairway runs along the floor of a valley between two steep hills. You can't even see the ocean."
"You can from the hills."

"Would you consider yourself to be a poor golfer or a really poor golfer?" a pro asked a student.
"Really poor," the student replied. "If I were just poor, I wouldn't be bothered with lessons."

"I actually enjoy golfing with bifocal glasses," a golfer said to the others in his foursome. "When I tee up my ball, I look through the bottom and it appears to be closer, and after I hit it I look through the top and it appears to go farther."

"A picture is worth a thousand words," a wife was informed.
"Not with my husband's golf," she replied. "With him, a thousand words can give you a pretty good picture."

An Englishman was visiting a city in North America where it had been drizzling steady for more than a week. His host was about to cancel the golf date they had planned when the Englishman said, "It's nice to see we at least have good weather."

"Which sport do you enjoy the most?" a golfer was asked.
"Golf," he answered.
"Why?" he was asked.
"You know," the golfer replied, "I often ask myself that very same question."

"I wanted to get out on the course and play a round before everything I learned in practice escaped me," one golfer said to another on the first tee.
As his ball sailed over a fence, another golfer commented, "I think it's already escaped."

Do you think it's fair that a bad golf game lasts longer than a good golf game?

"When I first began golfing," a woman said, "I was a very analytical golfer. I would logically rationalize my swing, and systematically set out to make corrections so that I could improve my game, but I don't have to do that any more."
"Have you improved that much?"
"No. Now my husband does it for me."

"My new instructional technique will have you shooting below a hundred in no time," an instructor said following a student's first lesson.
The student guffawed. "I'm already shooting below a hundred."
The instructor's face lit up. "See, it's working already."

"I can't decide whether to hit it straight away, draw it to the left, or fade it to the right," a golfer remarked as he teed up his ball.
"Is he really that good?" one onlooker said to another.
"No," the other onlooker replied. "It's just that this way, no matter where it goes, he has a reason for it."

A lot of golfers try to show everyone how good they are. A lot of golfers try to conceal it.

"Do you ever have trouble remembering which club to use on each hole?" one wife asked another.
"No," the second wife answered.
"How do you do it?" the first wife asked.
"It's not too difficult," the second wife replied, then she turned toward her husband and said, "Honey, which club should I use on this hole?"

"Why is it professional golfers manage to remember their strokes, and we don't?"
"If one of our strokes was worth half a million dollars, you can bet we'd remember it."

One golfer shot a low score by playing two off the tee, three out of the rough, one out of a lake, and three more out of a sand trap. He then four putted for par.

A golfer bought $3000 worth of golf clubs, a $500 bag, $60 golf balls, and $600 worth of shoes and clothing. He says they allow him to play his own game.

"That was a fair shot," a bystander told a golfer. The golfer beamed. "Why thank you! Thank you very much!"
"Telling you that you're *just fair* isn't much of a compliment to get so excited about," another golfer informed him.
"It is when you're as bad as I am," the first golfer responded.

"What's that new golfer doing out on the highway?" one golfer asked another.
"It could be my fault," the second golfer replied. "He asked me if he had to hit his ball from where it landed, and I said yes. I should have mentioned that there were some exceptions."

First golfer: "I make my tee times for the morning because I think I play better then." Second golfer: "I make my tee times for the afternoon because I think I play better then." Third golfer: "I make my tee times for morning and afternoon, just to be on the safe side."

"My golf game is constantly changing."
"Is it getting better or worse?"
"Yes."

A golfer, who had dug many holes in bunkers while unsuccessfully attempting to blast golf balls out of the sand, was signing up for a tournament.
"First name?" the clerk asked.
"Lawrence," he replied.
"Last name?" the clerk continued.
"Of Arabia," another golfer answered.

Some school children were playing a game called '*Who Am I*'.
"Neither rain nor snow nor gloom of night will keep me from my appointed rounds," a mail carrier's son said. "Who am I?"
"A golfer," another boy replied.

One golfer has a sure fire way to speed up the game. Charge by the hour.

A hardy foursome had slopped through eleven holes of golf on a course that had been drenched by a week of torrential rains. Finally, they could go no farther because of a creek that had overflowed its banks and completely covered the twelfth green and surrounding area.
As they surveyed the flood, one of the golfers commented, "This must be the water hole they were telling us about."

The secret to good golf is the swing. Take a few swings and you'll realize why they call it a secret.

Two wives were discussing how they met their husbands.
"I met my husband for the first time while golfing," said one wife, "and boy, was he cussing and swearing."
"Because he was not having a good game?" said the other wife.
"No," the first wife replied. "Because I hit him with my golf ball."

The golfers in a foursome were moaning about their poor drives.
"My ball missed the fairway and went into the rough," said one.
"My ball missed the rough and went into the lake," said the second.
"My ball even missed the lake," said the third. "I think it went out onto the street."
They all looked at the fourth golfer who was getting ready to tee off. "Don't look at me," he exclaimed. "I'm afraid to hit mine."

"My five iron prevented me from hitting the green," a golfer complained.
"Why your five iron?"
"That's what I was using."

"As I stand here on this first tee," a golfer philosophized, "I can't help but be struck by the wonderment of golf."
"You mean, how we manage to hit this little ball?" another golfer asked.
"No, no, not that," the philosopher replied as he watched his first drive of the day sail into a lake. "I mean, *why* we would want to hit this little ball."

"My wife is an extremely cautious golfer. Not only does she check to make sure there is no one in the fairway ahead, she checks the fairways on both sides."

"I can't believe the price of this drink," a golfer said to the young woman on the refreshment cart. "It's as much as I paid for my tee time."
"What!" she exclaimed. "No tip!"

"Why do you continue to take lessons from that instructor?" one golfer asked another who was not improving.
"I have to have somebody to blame my game on," the first golfer replied.

"I had a very pleasant surprise the other day."
"You managed to shoot par . . . ?"
"No."
"You managed to hit a green . . . ?"
"No."
"You managed to hit a fairway . . . ?"
"No."
"What . . . ????"
"I managed to get a tee time."

"As egos go, my husband has a very good one," one wife said to another. "Unfortunately, his ego is a better golfer than he is."

A beginner was shooting eights and nines and tens and elevens, then he came to a difficult par five hole and shot a fifteen.
"Heck," he said. "Anybody can have one bad hole."

First golfer: "Where is that great shot you were going to pull out of your bag and show me?"
Second golfer: "I left it in the bag."

"Which hole are you going for?" a forgetful golfer was asked by a grounds keeper who found him wandering around in the rough. "Number six or number seven?"
"Which direction was I walking when you met me?" the forgetful golfer responded.
"That way," he was told. "Toward number seven."
"Number seven it must be then," he answered as he dropped another ball and prepared to take a swing.

"Did my ball land in the rough or the fairway?" one golfer asked another.
"I'm not sure," the other golfer replied. "Which area of the golf course is that lake considered to be part of?"

Golf etiquette: Letting another golfer finish bragging about his game before you begin bragging about your own game.

Why do they call the rough, the rough? Why don't they just call it what it is, that tall crap to stay out of.

For some strange reason, the golf swing seems to work better for golfers who work at their golf swing.

The foursome had not spoken a word in sixteen holes. Finally, after one of them hit a drive to within two feet of the pin, another said, "Good shot."
To which a third responded, "Did we come here to talk or to golf."

Why is it, when I aim for the green I hit the rough, when I aim for the fairway I hit the rough, when I aim for the rough I still hit the rough. You would think if I aimed for the rough I would hit something else.

I began to realize that perhaps I wasn't the best golfer in the world when I discovered I could get to my ball faster by walking than by taking the electric golf cart.

"I was going to take my new girlfriend golfing on our first date, but my father advised against it. He said that all the members of our family were such poor golfers, and had such bad tempers on the golf course, that I would surely embarrass myself."
"He said that if I really wanted to impress a young lady with my social graces, that I should take her some place more elegant, where people were civilized, where I could introduce her to a more dignified class of society, some place where they had at least partially mastered the rules of etiquette."
"So where did you take her?"
"Bowling."

"My husband purchased a new driver this morning, and he's already at the practice range trying it out."
"Why the hurry?"
"He said he wanted to use it at least once before it became obsolete."

"My golf game isn't as good as it used to be. I'm just not playing enough. I think I'm going to have to get out on the course more often."
"Just how bad is your game?"
"Well, from Sunday to Thursday it wasn't too bad, but Friday and Saturday . . . ."

One golfer shot a low score the hard way, with his golf clubs.

"Why are you laughing at your golfing partner? The poor fellow sliced his ball into the lake."
"It's his own fault. First he laughed, and then I laughed."
"You mean he laughed when he hit his ball into the lake?"
"No. He laughed when I hit my ball into the lake."

"I finally found the gene that determines whether a human being will become a golfer," one scientist said to another.
"Really? Where is it?" the other scientist asked.
"I don't know," the first scientist replied. "I never seem to find it in the same place twice."

"I wonder," one golfer said to another after four putting, "could putter be short for putterer?"

There is nothing we can do about losing some of our golfing skills as we grow older. Our sense of humor, now that we should hold on to. The happiest golfers retain their sense of humor.

Two artists were golfing.
One says, "How's your score?"
The other looks at his card and replies, "I think I'm going to have to touch it up a little."

A golfer who was 35 over par by the seventh hole, hadn't hit a fairway all day, and had just driven his ball 100 feet into the rough, asked, "Do you think I should use a five or a six here?"

"Why are you upset?" one golfer asked another. "Because I keep thinking about the rotten golf I'm going to be playing for the next twenty years," the other golfer replied.
"What makes you think you're going to play *rotten* golf for the next twenty years?"
"Oh, I don't know, unless it could be the *rotten* golf I've played for the past twenty years."

One golfer was so tired of losing golf balls that he gave up the game and became a bowler. They lost his bowling ball.

First golfer: "Let us give thanks."
Second golfer: "O.K. I'm thankful I'm a golfer."
Third golfer: "I'm thankful I'm able to hit a golf ball."
Fourth golfer: "I'm thankful I don't own a house along the side of this fairway."

"I'm not saying that he has an affinity for getting his golf balls wet," a golfer said after another member of his foursome had driven three balls into a lake, "but he once hit a water truck going by on the highway."

"Last month my golf instructor said I should practice with each club until my shots become consistent, and then move on to another club, so that's what I'm doing."
"Which club did you begin with?"
"My three iron."
"And which club are you using now?"
"My three iron."

The more I know about golf, the more I know I don't know about golf.

"The other golfers in our foursome say they couldn't get along without me."
"Because you're so good and know so much about the game?"
"Because I'm the only one with a ball retriever."

"See those golfers standing in the middle of the green adding up their score cards? I'll bet I can make them move in two seconds."
"Bet you can't."
"Bet I can."
"How?"
"FORE!!!!"

"My wife and I had a strange and wondrous golf game today," a husband confided to some friends. "She hit a lot of strange shots that somehow ended up on the green, and I'm still wondering how she did that."

"What was your score?" a golfer was asked.
"72," he replied.
After enduring several seconds of the other golfers staring at him, he said, "Oh, all right, 97."

Very few people believe a golfer when he tells them his score, which is understandable, since he's usually talking to other golfers.

Two golf course owners were discussing their investment.
"I think we might have made a mistake hiring that architect to design our new course," said one of the owners.
"Why?" asked the other.
"Because I don't think he has the experience we thought he had."
"What makes you say that?"
"He submitted drawings for nineteen holes."

A patient went to a doctor with a sore back. "It's caused by your golf swing," said the doctor. "I've had the same problem myself, and I can tell you from experience that the only way to get rid of your sore back is to give up golf for a month."
"But I'm not a golfer," the patient informed him.
"In that case," the doctor responded, "I don't know what will help you."

Why, after twenty years of golfing, do we still have those games that make us feel like it's our first time on the course.

"Does your wife get angry when she hits a ball into a lake?" a husband was asked.
"Sometimes she gets a little angry," he replied.
"What about when she hits two balls into a lake?"
"She might get a little angrier."
"What about when she hits three balls into a lake?"
"She doesn't seem to get any angrier."
"How can you tell?"
"I heard her say so."
"What did she say?"
"She said, I can't get any angrier."

"It's tough teeing off on the first hole in front of such a huge audience."
"What do you mean, a huge audience? There are only seven other golfers watching."
"Believe me, when you're teeing off on the first hole, that's a huge audience."

A golfer, who was not having a very good day, walked off the seventeenth green after recording an eight on the hole.
A newer member of the foursome, overlooking the golfer's obvious problems with his game, asked, "Which is your favorite hole on this course?"
"Probably the eighteenth," the golfer replied.
"Why the eighteenth?" the newcomer inquired.
"Because I haven't played it yet," the golfer responded.

"Why do you golf so much?"
"My mother. When I was a little boy, she told me to eat my vegetables. She said, you might not like them and you will probably never want to see them again, but in spite of your temper tantrums, they're good for you. I've applied the same philosophy to golf."

"The biggest problem with my golf game appears to be coordination between left and right," a golfer announced. "My hook to the left doesn't know what my slice to the right is doing."

Some golfers sure are funny. They still manage to have a good time even though all their golf balls end up in the rough or a lake, and they haven't hit a green in five years.

"I have some good news and some bad news," a golf course manager informed the course owner.
"Give me the bad news," the owner said.
"Since you've stopped spending money," the manager replied, "the course is in the worst condition I've ever seen. The grass hasn't been cut in the fairways, the greens are brown, the lakes have turned to mud, it's deplorable."
"And what's the good news?"
"We've still selling every tee time."

"I just can't bring myself to join that golf and country club."
"Don't like it?"
"Can't afford it."

Keep in mind, before you begin telling other golfers how great you are, they might want to see some proof.

The really great golfers tell us about their game. The rest of us have to actually play the game.

A golfer who played six days a week was told that anyone who golfed that many times must be missing something in his life, so he began golfing seven days a week.

A golfer is a person who can't golf, who brags about his game to other golfers who can't golf.

"What did you shoot today?" an old timer was asked.
"70," he answered without hesitation.
"How do you know you shot 70?" the other golfer demanded. "You didn't even fill out a score card."
"Didn't have to," the old timer replied. "When I first started playing, I shot 140, and I figure I'm at least twice as good now as I was then."

"Using my new system, no matter how badly I play, I refuse to give myself more than 10 strokes on any one hole."
"Really? And using your new system, what was your score in your game today?"
"180."

"Could you tell me which is the best part of this green to aim for?" a golfer unfamiliar with the course asked another golfer.
"I'm afraid I can't help you there," the other golfer answered.
"Why not?" the offended newcomer asked.
"I've never hit this green," the other golfer responded.

After a golfer's first three drives went into a lake, and his fourth went into the rough, he cheerfully exclaimed, "Well, at least I'm getting better."

"Did you see my last shot?" said an overbearing golfer who was constantly bragging about his game.
"Unfortunately, I don't think we have," another golfer whispered to his playing partner.

"Your golf swing reminds me of Palmer."
"The famous golfer?"
"No. My brother, the hockey player."

A golfer was retrieving his golf ball from a lake when he spotted a few other balls. He decided he might as well retrieve them too. He had hauled out an additional four or five when he noticed some other golfers watching. He looked at them, then looked at the golf balls and exclaimed, "They're not *all* mine."

One professional golfer is trying to get the other golfers to unionize. He thinks they should be paid overtime for Saturday and Sunday.

"I suppose what goes down must come up," a golfer sighed as his towering drive landed in the middle of a lake.
"Don't you mean, what goes up must come down?" another golfer responded.
"No," he said. "I mean what goes down must come up."
"You are talking about your ball, aren't you?"
"No. My score."

"What makes you enjoy golf so much?"
"Determination and devotion."
"Determination and devotion would certainly make a person a better golfer."
"I wasn't talking about the golf. I was talking about the enjoyment."

It was extremely windy on the course today. Depending on which direction I was going, and how high I hit the ball, the distance of my drives varied considerably. One went three hundred yards. Another went minus ten.

"Do you think I will make a good golfer?" a student asked.
"I certainly do," the instructor answered.
"How good do you think I will be?"
"The best."
"Do you think I will someday be good enough to shoot par?"
"Absolutely."
"What about turning pro someday?"
"I don't see why not."
"Boy oh boy, then I'm ready to get started."
"Good. Now the first thing we have to learn is, you hold the other end of the club."

"I do very well golfing, except for just two areas on the course."
"Which two areas?"
"The front nine and the back nine."

"Do you know what happens when a golfer allows his head to be turned by his ego?"
"He sees where his slices are going . . . ?"

"What's your handicap?" a golfer was asked.
"Twenty," he answered, "and I have a difficult time keeping it there."
"What do you mean, difficult time keeping it there? You were only seven over par in the last tournament you played, and you won that."
"I know. Why do you think I have such a difficult time keeping it at twenty."

"I promise you'll have a whole new golf game after you finish your lessons," a golf pro assured a student.
"How much of an improvement do you think I'll see?" asked the student.
"I didn't mention anything about improvement," the pro replied. "I just said new."

A professional golfer gave up the game to become a man of the cloth. After several weeks of trying to encourage parishioners to attend services, he was heard to comment, "I think I might have finally found something that's more difficult than golf."

Boring golfer: One who insists on talking about his game when you want to talk about yours.

Two professionals were examining the lie of their golf balls which had landed near each other in deep rough. The grass was wet from a drizzling rain, their clothing was soaked, and they saw no way of getting out without a penalty and a drop. One turned to the other and said, "And they tell us we're supposed to be the *best* golfers . . . ."

"My husband tried to get me interested in golf," one wife said to another. "But I just couldn't. Golf puts me to sleep."
"So, a lot of people fall asleep watching golf," the other wife answered.
"But I wasn't watching it," the first wife replied. "I was playing it."

Why do the ducks on the golf course laugh at us? We're not all that funny, are we . . . ?

"Medically trained golf staff," a sign on the wall behind the clerk read.
"Why would you need a medically trained golf staff?" a golfer inquired.
"On the off chance we have to revive a fainting customer who comes in for a tee time," the clerk answered.
"When would you ever have to revive a fainting customer who comes in for a tee time?" the golfer asked.
"Every once in a while we have a tee time open," the clerk replied.

"You and I may not agree on how to hit the ball," one golfer said to another, "but we do agree on where to hit it. I'll help you look for yours if you'll help me look for mine."

"Golf helped me appreciate how great life can be without tension and stress."
"Golf got rid of your tension and stress?"
"I'm talking about after I gave up golf."

A golfer who practices doesn't get that much more out of the game of golf than a golfer who does practice . . . except possibly a lot more fun.

"What do you usually shoot on this course?" a golfer was asked.
"Just about par," the golfer answered.
The listener was impressed, until he watched the golfer shoot three over par on the first hole, then two over par on the second hole, and four over par on the third hole. The rest of his game was just about the same.
As the golfer finished up on the eighteenth hole with yet another three over par, the person who had asked the question was waiting. He was about to confront him when he heard the golfer say, "Well, that's just about par for this course."

"On this hole," one golfer said to another who was unfamiliar with the course, "there's a lake over there, and a sand trap over there, and deep rough over there."
"Uh huh," the second golfer offered. "And where's the green?"
"Hmm," the helpful golfer replied. "It must be in there somewhere."

First golfer: "I wonder if God has a golf course waiting for us in heaven."
Second golfer: "Not if there is a just God."

"We finally solved the problem of all the golfers missing the number five fairway," a golf course manager said.
"How?"
"We turned it sideways."

"I love golf," a golfer exclaimed, "and getting out on Saturday mornings, and hitting a few golf balls down the middle of the ol' fairway."
"Did he say *few* or *very few*?" another golfer commented.

"Which length driver would you prefer," a golfer was asked, "the one with the regular shaft, the long shaft, or the extra long shaft?"
"Let me see," the golfer replied. "I can hit the ball straighter with the regular length shaft, I can hit the ball farther with the long shaft, and even though I can't hit a fairway I get my longest drives with the extra long shaft. Give me the driver with the extra long shaft."

"Being a beginner is not a crime," a new golfer said.
"Well, it should be," a grumpy old golfer replied.

Have you ever wondered how the clerk in the pro shop always manages to give the slowest foursome of the day the tee time just ahead of yours?

My son always wanted to go golfing with me, even though he was still too young to be allowed on the course. I would often comfort him by giving him money for a movie.
When he was older I said, "Well, at last, you can go golfing."
He said, "I don't want to go golfing."
I said, "But you've wanted to go golfing with me for all these years."
He said, "No, I didn't. I just wanted money for a movie."

"This is the first time I ever hit my ball into a lake on the first fairway."
"How many golf courses have you played?"
"This is my first."

"One golfer's game is so bad he copies from other golfer's score cards."

Two very competitive golfers were talking.
"I think there was something wrong with my golf game today," one of them commented.
"What makes you say that?" the other asked.
"I found myself enjoying it," the first replied.

Two golfers were in the habit of subtracting a stroke here and there on their score cards, so to make sure they wouldn't cheat they agreed to keep score for each other. When they got their cards back, each had added five strokes.

We have yet to play with golfers who are as good as they would like to be.

A man was waiting at the pearly gates. He had a golf bag slung over his shoulder.
"What are you doing here?" Saint Peter said. "You're not due for another forty years."
"I know," the man replied, "but I took up golf, and I couldn't afford to live."

"My wife limits herself to one mulligan per game. Of course the number of strokes in her mulligan varies just a tad."

"I left my last golf instructor because he took all my money and didn't teach me anything," a golfer said to a club pro. "That won't happen here, will it?"
"Of course not."
"I'm certainly glad to hear that. Now, how much do you charge for a lesson?"
"How much do you have?"

I have not found any difference in the quality of golf clubs. I've tried hundreds, and not one of them has improved my game.

"Anything you need to know about this golf course, just ask me," one golfer said to another. "I know every rough, every lake, every sand trap, every hazard, I know every inch of it."
The other golfer was impressed. "Really?" he exclaimed. "How long have you been playing here?"
"Since this morning."

"How are playing conditions today?"
"Not too bad. The roughs are about three feet high. The fairways might be a little shorter."

A professional golfer made a tee time at a small town course and was placed in a group with three local golfers. Trying to be helpful, they pointed out where all the obstacles were.
"I'm afraid we've hit just about every rough and lake there is," one of them offered.
To which the professional golfer responded, "We have a lot in common."

An American and an Englishman were doing a little bragging about the sizes of golf courses in their respective countries. The lengths in their stories grew from 7000 yards, to 8000 yards, to 9000 yards and beyond.
Finally the American said, "We have one golf course in the United States that measures more than 2000 miles from east to west."
"Don't be ridiculous," the Englishman replied. "That would take you all the way to the Pacific Ocean."
"I know," glowed the American. "That's the water hole I was telling you about."

"My husband plays with a really old set of golf clubs."
"Which club is that he's using now?"
"An IX iron."

A foursome that had been held up for a considerable length of time by the slow group of golfers ahead, waited and watched as one by one they prepared to sink their putts. As each poky putter circled his golf ball, examined the line to the hole, went back and circled his ball again, and then repeated the procedure, a golfer in the waiting foursome commented, "I think it has finally happened."
"What?" another in the foursome asked.
The golfer sighed. "Chess and golf have finally merged."

My husband bought a computer golf program to help him get rid of his slice. After playing it for two weeks the computer developed a slice.

"I know a man who golfed all his life, then he stopped, and died. What do you think of that?"
"I think he should have kept golfing."

One of the more interesting sights in golf is watching golfers line up a drive or a putt . . . like it's actually going to go where they aim it . . . .

"Is that new golfer in our foursome any good?"
"I'll say. Everybody else has to play twice as good just to get the same score."

A golfer, who was not having a good round, was asked why she liked playing on that particular golf course.
With tongue in cheek she replied, "Because they keep the roughs in such wonderful condition."

Anger and golf don't mix. That's why I don't swear until after I take my shot.

One foursome golfs religiously, every Sunday morning.

Ask any golfer who they would rather play with, an experienced golfer or someone who keeps up. They will choose the golfer who keeps up.

If you can tell what your golf score is without looking at a score card, you are probably a very good golfer.

A good golf swing combines all the attributes of the fade and the draw. The trick is to combine them at the same time, so that your ball lands somewhere in between.

"I can't seem to find my swing today," a golfer complained.
"I seem to have found several of them," another golfer replied.

"Is this green difficult to hit?" one golfer asked another.
"It can't be too difficult," the other golfer replied. "The foursome on that other fairway have hit it twice."

* * * * * * * *

All my love to Sheila:

Sheila likes to help me decide which clothes I should wear when we go golfing.
"How come you choose my clothes now," I asked, "but when I used to go golfing by myself you let me wear anything I wanted?"
"Because I didn't have to be seen with you then," she answered.

Ron

500
ALL TIME FUNNIEST
A Collection Of Favorite Golf Jokes And Stories, By Golfers And About Golfers
GOLF
JOKES
STORIES, & FAIRWAY WISDOM
NO, I DID NOT LOSE MY BALL. IT'S IN THE MIDDLE OF THAT LAKE OVER THERE.
by Sheila & Ron Stewart

Volume II
500 MORE
ALL TIME FUNNIEST
Of Their Favorite Golf Jokes And Stories By Golfers And About Golfers
GOLF
JOKES
STORIES, & FAIRWAY WISDOM
I THINK YOUR FIRST DRIVE INTO THE ROUGH WAS A PRETTIER SHOT, BUT YOUR SECOND DRIVE INTO THE LAKE APPEARED TO GO FARTHER.
by Sheila & Ron Stewart

Another
500
ALL TIME FUNNIEST
Volume III
Of Their Favorite Golf Jokes & Stories, By Golfers & About Golfers
GOLF
JOKES
STORIES, & FAIRWAY WISDOM
IT LOOKS LIKE IT COULD BREAK A LITTLE TO THE LEFT OR MAYBE TO THE RIGHT.
by Sheila & Ron Stewart

500
Volume IV
Slightly Off The Fairway
ALL TIME FUNNIEST
GOLF
JOKES
STORIES, & FAIRWAY WISDOM
I WONDER IF THIS IS WHERE "TAKE A STROKE AND A DROP" CAME FROM
by Sheila & Ron Stewart

Volume V

Of Their All Time Favorite Golf Jokes And Stories By Golfers And About Golfers

500

ALL TIME FUNNIEST

HUSBAND & WIFE

GOLF JOKES

STORIES, & FAIRWAY WISDOM

AND THIS IS MY HUSBAND, HE'S TEACHING ME HOW TO GOLF.

by Sheila & Ron Stewart

If your local book store does not have a copy of 500 All Time Funniest Golf Jokes, Stories & Fairway Wisdom or our other books, we will be happy to let you know where you can acquire them, or fill your order direct.

Acadia Scale Press

Telephone: 480-496-6191

E-mail: books@acadiascale.com

www.ingramcontent.com/pod-product-compliance
Lightning Source LLC
Chambersburg PA
CBHW031256060726
47590CB00003B/930
* 9 7 8 0 9 6 5 6 8 5 6 2 7 *